S0-AXJ-022

Basic Telephone Training

A Basic Course in Telephone Language and Skills

Anne Watson-Delestrée

CONTEMPORARY BOOKS

a division of NTC/CONTEMPORARY PUBLISHING GROUP
Lincolnwood, Illinois USA

The Author
Anne Watson-Delestrée is a British teacher of English, living and working in Paris. She has years
of experience of ESP teaching. She developed this course for the many hundreds of students she
taught who needed to use and understand English on the telephone. In its initial form she used
this course successfully in many schools and companies in the Paris area. She is grateful for the
comments of all her colleagues over the years who piloted the material and offered suggestions.
In particular, she thanks Anne Pichon for her help, and colleagues at A.V.L. and Bull, Paris, for
piloting several units.

Interior illustrations: James Buckley

ISBN: 0-8092-0596-3

This edition first published 1999 Contemporary Books,
a division of NTC/Contemporary Publishing Group, Inc.,
4255 W. Touhy Avenue, Lincolnwood (Chicago), Illinois 60646-1975 U.S.A.
©1992 LTP
All rights reserved. No part of this book may be reproduced,
stored in a retrieval system, or transmitted in any form or by any means,
electronic, mechanical, photocopying, recording, or otherwise,
without prior permission of NTC/Contemporary Publishing Group, Inc.
Manufactured in the United States of America.

90 RCP 0987654321

Basic Telephone Training

A Basic Course in Telephone Language and Skills

Anne Watson-Delestrée

CONTEMPORARY BOOKS

a division of NTC/CONTEMPORARY PUBLISHING GROUP
Lincolnwood, Illinois USA

The Author
Anne Watson-Delestrée is a British teacher of English, living and working in Paris. She has years
of experience of ESP teaching. She developed this course for the many hundreds of students she
taught who needed to use and understand English on the telephone. In its initial form she used
this course successfully in many schools and companies in the Paris area. She is grateful for the
comments of all her colleagues over the years who piloted the material and offered suggestions.
In particular, she thanks Anne Pichon for her help, and colleagues at A.V.L. and Bull, Paris, for
piloting several units.

Interior illustrations: James Buckley

ISBN: 0-8092-0596-3

This edition first published 1999 Contemporary Books,
a division of NTC/Contemporary Publishing Group, Inc.,
4255 W. Touhy Avenue, Lincolnwood (Chicago), Illinois 60646-1975 U.S.A.
©1992 LTP
All rights reserved. No part of this book may be reproduced,
stored in a retrieval system, or transmitted in any form or by any means,
electronic, mechanical, photocopying, recording, or otherwise,
without prior permission of NTC/Contemporary Publishing Group, Inc.
Manufactured in the United States of America.

90 RCP 0987654321

To the Teacher   v

To the Student   vi

BASIC TELEPHONE LANGUAGE

Unit 1   Starting the Call   1

Unit 2   The Boss Is Out   4

Unit 3   The Wrong Number   7

Unit 4   A Bad Connection   10

Unit 5   Answering Machines   12

Unit 6   Number Review   14

Unit 7   Telephone Numbers   16

Unit 8   The Date   19

Unit 9   Telling Time   22

Unit 10   Spelling Clearly   25

Unit 11   Taking Down an Address   29

Unit 12   Prepositions   32

Unit 13   Basic Language Review   38

BASIC TELEPHONE SKILLS

Unit 14a	Listening Practice	43
14b	Getting the Message	44
Unit 15a	Listening Practice	45
15b	Getting the Message	46
Unit 16a	Listening Practice	47
16b	Getting the Message	48
Unit 17a	Listening Practice	49
17b	Getting the Message	50
Unit 18a	Listening Practice	51
18b	Getting the Message	52
Unit 19a	Listening Practice	53
19b	Getting the Message	54
Unit 20a	Listening Practice	55
20b	Getting the Message	56
Unit 21a	Listening Practice	57
21b	Getting the Message	58
Unit 22a	Listening Practice	59
22b	Getting the Message	60
Unit 23a	Listening Practice	61
23b	Getting the Message	62
Unit 24a	Listening Practice	63
24b	Getting the Message	64
Unit 25a	Listening Practice	65
25b	Getting the Message	66
Unit 26a	Listening Practice	67
26b	Getting the Message	68
Unit 27a	Listening Practice	69
27b	Getting the Message	70
Unit 28a	Listening Practice	71
28b	Getting the Message	72
	Answer Key	73

To the Teacher

THE COURSE

This course consists of the student's book and cassette tape. It is designed to be used in class or as self-study material. The comprehensive key includes the script of all recorded material not printed in the individual student units.

THE AIM

The title *Basic Telephone Training* speaks for itself. The course is designed to make elementary students efficient telephone users within a limited area. At the end of this course, students should be able to cope with the telephone duties of a receptionist or switchboard operator.

THE STRUCTURE OF THE COURSE

The course is in two parts:
Units 1–13: Basic Telephone Language
These units teach the necessary functional phrases and vocabulary. This includes crucial areas such as numbers, dates, and prepositions, where accuracy is essential.
Units 14–28: Basic Telephone Skills
1. Listening: the A pages of these units
2. Taking messages: the B pages
3. Speaking: the role-play Phone Play sections

TEACHING THE COURSE

You can work through the course unit by unit or you can alternate units from the language section with units from the skills section. Lower-level students should not start the skills section until they have completed most if not all of the language section.

ROLE-PLAY PHONE PLAYS

These are information-gap pair work exercises. It is excellent if students can use telephones and sit in different rooms. If this is impossible, ask students to sit in pairs, back to back, and perform the Phone Plays without looking at each other.

SPEAKING ON THE TELEPHONE

Learning to speak a new language is difficult. Learning to speak it on the telephone—when you cannot see the caller—is even more difficult. This course teaches you to listen, to speak, and to take messages.

THE DIALOGUES

All the dialogues are on tape. Listen to them once or twice, sometimes looking at your book, sometimes just listening. When you repeat after the tape, try not to look at your book. Do this several times until you sound natural. Then read the dialogue aloud without the tape.

DIFFERENT ACCENTS

The people on the tape have different accents. When you use the telephone at work, everyone has a different accent!

THE EXERCISES

All the answers to the exercises are in the answer key at the end of the book. Try to do an exercise without looking at the key. If you find an exercise difficult, look at the key, but close the key before you write the answers.

LEARNING AT HOME

If you are studying this course at home without a teacher, here is some advice especially for you:
1. Do not be afraid to use the key—the key is your teacher.
2. Do not try to go too fast. Finish one unit before starting the next. Make sure you understand everything in one unit before you begin the next.
3. Try to do some of the units from the skills section while you are studying Units 1–13.
4. Decide on a timetable for studying and stick to it!

Starting the Call

EXERCISE 1

Listen to this conversation. Repeat after the tape.

> You: Good morning. CPA Corporation.
>
> Caller: Hello. I'd like to speak to Mr. Martin, please.
>
> You: Who's calling, please?
>
> Caller: This is John Bush of Lion Computers.
>
> You: One moment, please. I'll connect you. Go ahead, Mr. Bush.

Tip Don't just answer *Hello*. Give your name.

EXERCISE 2

Here are other phrases you can use. Put them in the correct order to make a conversation. Read them aloud, then listen to this dialogue on tape.

_____ **a.** May I speak to Mr. Martin, please?

_____ **b.** One moment, please. I'm connecting you.

_____ **c.** John Bush of Lion Computers.

_____ **d.** Accounting Department. May I help you?

_____ **e.** Who's calling?

EXERCISE 3

Fill in the blanks in this conversation with information from your company.

> You: _____. Good morning.
>
> Caller: May I speak to _____, please?
>
> You: _____, please _____.

EXERCISE 4

Listen to the tape. Fill in the blanks in these conversations.

1. You: _____ Interface. May I help you?

    Caller: Hello. _____ I speak to Mr. Stevenson, please?

    You: _____ moment, please. I'm

    _____.

2. You: _____ PLC International.

    Caller: _____ speak to Mr. Davies, please.

    You: Who's _____, please?

    Caller: _____ Charles Williamson of Micro Logics.

    You: _____, please. I'll _____.

EXERCISE 5

Write expressions that mean the same thing as the ones below. The first one is done for you.

Belfry Consultants. May I help you? *Good morning. Belfry*
Consultants.

I'd like to speak to Mr. Brown, please. _____

_____

Who's speaking, please? _____

_____

This is Brian Howard of Jason's. _____

_____

Hold on, Mr. Howard. _____

_____

I'll put you through. _____

_____

EXERCISE 6

Look at this telephone number. Someone is calling from the United States to Tokyo, Japan.

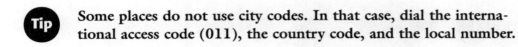

011	81	3	44 69 32
international access code	country code	city code	local telephone number

Tip Some places do not use city codes. In that case, dial the international access code (011), the country code, and the local number.

Look in your own telephone directory for the correct codes to the countries below.

1. Australia _____ 2. India _____

3. Brazil _____ 4. Mexico _____

Tip Long-distance calls within the United States use *area codes.*

Look in your own telephone directory. Find the area codes for the cities below.

5. Los Angeles _____ 6. Washington D.C. _____

7. Chicago _____ 8. Atlanta _____

Unit 2

The Boss Is Out

Listen to this conversation. Repeat after the tape.

> You: Digital Electronics. Good afternoon.
>
> Caller: May I speak to Mr. Burton, please?
>
> You: I'm sorry, but Mr. Burton is in a meeting. May I take a message?
>
> Caller: That's all right. What time will he be available?
>
> You: At 3 o'clock.
>
> Caller: Could you tell him I called? It's Mr. Rees.
>
> You: Certainly.
>
> Caller: Thank you very much. Good-bye.
>
> You: Good-bye.

Tip *Certainly* means *yes* and is very friendly.

EXERCISE

Here are other phrases you can use. Put the lines in the correct order to make a conversation. Read them aloud. Then listen to this dialogue on tape.

_____ **a.** That's all right. When will she be back?

_____ **b.** Certainly, Mr. Blair.

_____ **c.** Walker and Williams. Good morning.

_____ **d.** Thanks for your help.

_____ **e.** Please tell her I called.

_____ **f.** I'm sorry, but she's out at the moment.

_____ **g.** You're welcome. Good-bye.

_____ **h.** May I speak to Mrs. Blair, please? I'm Mr. Blair.

_____ **i.** I'm afraid I don't know.

Tip *I'm afraid* can mean *I'm sorry.* Use *I'm afraid* to give bad or negative information.

EXERCISE 3

Listen to the tape. Fill in the blanks in these conversations:

1.   You: I'm _____ Mr. Jones is

                 _____.

         Caller: Oh dear! _____ will he be

                 _____?

         You: At about _____.

         Caller: Well, could you _____, please?

2.   You: Hello. I'm _____, but Gloria is

                 _____. May I _____?

         Caller: No, that's all right. Could you just _____?

EXERCISE 4

This conversation doesn't sound natural. Rewrite it so that it sounds more natural and friendly.

         You: Hello. José Vidal here. _____

         Caller: Mrs. Rossi, please. _____

         You: Mrs. Rossi's not here. You call back? _____

                 _____

         Caller: What time? _____

         You: About 20 minutes. _____

         Caller: Thank you. _____

         You: It's OK. _____

 Tip Did you notice that you *added* extra phrases to make the information sound better?

EXERCISE 5

Listen to the tape. Fill in the correct day of the week in the sentences below.

1. He won't be back until _____ morning.

2. We open again on _____ morning at 9:00.

3. We will be closed from _____ the 16th until

    _____ the 18th.

4. The best time to call is before lunch on _____ or

    after 5:00 P.M. on _____.

EXERCISE 6

Look at this calendar. Today is the 16th. Write the dates in the blanks below.

AUGUST						
Sun	Mon	Tue	Wed	Thur	Fri	Sat
	1	2	3	4	5	6
7	8	9	10	11	12	13
14	15	16	17	18	19	20
21	22	23	24	25	26	27
28	29	30	31			

1. today _____

2. tomorrow _____

3. yesterday _____

4. a week from today _____

5. a week from tomorrow _____

6. last Tuesday _____

7. two weeks from tomorrow _____

 Tip   In English, don't say *7 or 8 days* or *14 or 15 days*. Say *a week* or *two weeks*.

Unit 3

The Wrong Number

EXERCISE 1

Listen to this conversation. Repeat after the tape.

> You: Hello. Amax Incorporated. Can I help you?
>
> Caller: May I speak to Mr. Rose, please?
>
> You: I'm sorry. There's nobody here by that name. I think you've got the wrong number.
>
> Caller: I'm sorry to have bothered you. Good-bye.
>
> You: Good-bye.

 Tip Note that you said, "<u>I think</u> you've got the wrong number." This sounds better than "You've got the wrong number," which is less polite.

EXERCISE 2

Here are other phrases you can use. Put the lines in the correct order to make a conversation. Read them aloud, then listen to this dialogue on tape.

_____ **a.** Good morning. Jameston and Associates.

_____ **b.** Oh, I'm very sorry. I must have the wrong number. Good-bye.

_____ **c.** Is this 553-9562?

_____ **d.** Good-bye.

_____ **e.** No, this is 553-9762.

EXERCISE 3

This caller has reached you, but he was calling someone else. Fill in the blanks with information about your company.

Caller: Is this Tell Brothers?

You: No, this is _____ .

Caller: I'd like to speak to Miss Van Hertzen, please.

You: I'm sorry. There's _____ .

Caller: Is this 489-9929?

You: No, _____ .

EXERCISE 4

Listen to this conversation. Then fill in the blanks.

You: Good afternoon. Susan McQueen speaking.

Caller: Is _____ extension 584?

You: No, this is extension 554. I'll _____ you to the switchboard.

Caller: Thanks for your help.

You: That's all right. Good-bye.

EXERCISE 5

First look at the information. Then listen to the tape and write your reply.

1. (Your name is Dorothy Smith.) _____

_____

2. (Your number is 992-4097.) _____

_____

3. (Your name is Mr. Reynolds.) _____

_____

EXERCISE 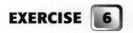 6

Put this conversation in the correct order. The first line is correct.

_1_   **a.** Could I speak to Mary Stone, please?

_____   **b.** No, this is extension 1245. Which department is she in?

_____   **c.** Thanks for your help. I'm sorry to have bothered you.
Good-bye.

_____   **d.** I'll put you through to her department.

_____   **e.** Training.

_____   **f.** That's all right. Good-bye.

_____   **g.** Oh, isn't this extension 1235?

_____   **h.** There's nobody here by that name, I'm afraid.

A Bad Connection

EXERCISE 1

Listen to this conversation. Repeat the phrases after the tape.

You: Good afternoon. First National Bank.

Caller: This is Sarah Patterson speaking.

You: Sorry?

Caller: This is Sarah Patterson of Bestcorp.

You: I'm sorry, but the connection is very bad. Please speak up.

Caller: This is Sarah Patterson in the Accounting Department of Bestcorp in Ohio.

You: I'm sorry, but I still can't hear you. This connection is very bad. Could you please call back?

EXERCISE 2

Practice saying these phrases after the tape.

1. **When you can't hear, say:**
   Sorry?
   Pardon?
   I can't hear you. The connection is very bad.
   Please speak up.

2. **When you don't understand, say:**
   I'm sorry, but I don't understand.
   Sorry, but I still don't understand.
   Please speak more slowly.

3. **When you are not sure, say:**
   Could you repeat that, please?
   Could you spell that, please?
   Please confirm by fax.

 Use *sorry* on the phone when you have a problem of some kind, when you don't understand, or when you can't hear.

EXERCISE 3

Listen to the tape. Fill in the blanks in the conversation below.

Caller: This is Paul Downs speaking.

You: _____?

Caller: Paul Downs speaking.

You: _____, but the connection is very bad.

Caller: PAUL DOWNS.

You: Could you _____ that, _____?

Caller: P–A–U–L D–O–W–N–S.

You: Could you _____ that, please?

Caller: P–A–U–L D–O–W–N–S.

You: _____, but I _____
don't understand.

Caller: P–A–U—

You: Ah, good afternoon, Mr. Downs. How are you?

EXERCISE 4

Use the clues below to fill in the puzzle.

1. Sorry? or _____?

     __ __ __ |D| __ __ __

2. You're speaking too quickly.
   Please speak more _____.

     __ __ |O| __ __ __

3. I don't _____.

     __ |N,| __ __ __ __ __ __ __ __

4. I _____ don't understand.

     __ |T| __ __ __

5. Speak more loudly. Please
   speak _____.

     __ |P| __ __

6. Say that again. Could you
   _____ that, please?

     __ __ __ __ |A| __

7. I don't speak _____ very well.

     __ |N| __ __ __ __ __

8. The _____ is very bad.
   I can't hear you.

     __ __ __ __ __ __ |I| __ __ __

9. Please _____ by fax.

     |C| __ __ __ __ __ __

Unit 5

Answering Machines

EXERCISE 1

Here are five different messages. Listen to each one on the tape. Then read it aloud. Record it yourself on a blank cassette.

1. General information
   You have reached All Africa Export, Incorporated. We're open from 9:00 A.M. to 6:00 P.M. Monday through Friday. Thank you for calling.

2. Office closed
   This is Duquoin International. Our office is currently closed. Please leave your name and phone number and we'll return your call as soon as possible. Speak after the tone.

3. Holding message
   Thank you for calling Transglobal Airways. Your call is important to us and will be answered in the order in which it was received. We apologize for the delay.

4. Informal message
   This is John Bach's office. I'm not in at the moment, but I'll call you back when I return. Please leave your name and number after the beep. Thanks for calling.

5. Fax Instructions message
   This is Agri-Cultura. The office is closed for vacation for two weeks. We reopen on Monday the 18th. If you have an urgent message, you may fax us at 555-2626. Again, that's fax number 555-2626.

EXERCISE 2

Look again at the messages above. Write any useful phrases (phrases you think you can use) on the lines below.

_____

_____

_____

_____

EXERCISE

Use the information below to write three messages. Use your name and/or the name of your company.

1. You're going to a meeting and won't be back in the office till tomorrow.

_____

_____

_____

2. It's 6 o'clock. You're going home.

_____

_____

_____

3. Your office is closing at lunchtime today. Business as usual tomorrow.

_____

_____

_____

EXERCISE 4

Listen to the tape. Fill in the blanks in these messages.

1. This is _____, Inc. Please _____.

We're sorry to _____.

2. This is Henry Barber's office. I'm _____ right now,

but if you leave me _____ and your phone

number, I'll _____ when I return. Please speak

_____.

Unit 6

Number Review

EXERCISE 1

Listen to the numbers on tape. Make sure you can say them all.

0	1	2	3	4	5	6	7	8	9
10	11	12	13	14	15	16	17	18	19
20	21	22	23						
30	40	50	60	70	80	90	100		

101 - one hundred one   111 - one hundred eleven

1,000 - one thousand   100,000 - one hundred thousand

1,000,000 - one million

EXERCISE 2

Look at these examples. Say them after the tape.

78	seventy-eight
425	four hundred twenty-five
1,210	one thousand, two hundred ten
48,601	forty-eight thousand, six hundred one
939,837	nine hundred thirty-nine thousand, eight hundred thirty-seven

EXERCISE 3

Write these numbers in words.

1. 51 _____

2. 812 _____

3. 4,739 _____

4. 204,110 _____

EXERCISE 4

Write these numbers in numerals.

1. twenty-eight thousand, nine hundred fourteen _____

2. seven hundred four _____

3. two thousand, three hundred fifty-one _____

4. six hundred thirty-four thousand, four hundred five _____

EXERCISE 5

Listen to the tape and fill in this puzzle.

Unit 7

Telephone Numbers

EXERCISE

Listen to these dialogues. Then repeat them after the tape.

1. Caller: Could you give me Mr. Hansen's home number, please?

    You: Yes, it's a different area code: three . . . two . . . nine . . . five . . .

    five . . . five . . . nine . . . oh . . . six . . . six.

    Caller: (329) 555-9066?

    You: That's right.

2. You: Baker and Williams. Good morning.

    Caller: Could I have extension 132, please?

    You: Who's calling?

    Caller: Helen DeWitt.

    You: One moment, please. I'll put you through.

Tips
> Say numbers separately. Say "three . . . seven . . . four."
> Pause between groups. Say "325 . . . 651." Say "89 . . . 44 . . . 90."
> For 0, say "oh."
> For 66, say "six . . . six."
> For 666, say "six . . . six . . . six."
> For 4981 Ext. 242, say: "four . . . nine . . . eight . . . one, extension two four two."
> For (312) 012-4414, the *area code* is 312 and the *phone number* is 012-4414.

EXERCISE 2

Listen to the tape and correct these numbers.

1. (217) 555-9567 _____

2. (601) 012-4658 _____

3. (305) 120-5133 _____

4. (414) 555-0284 _____

EXERCISE 3

Listen to the tape and write the correct extension numbers below.

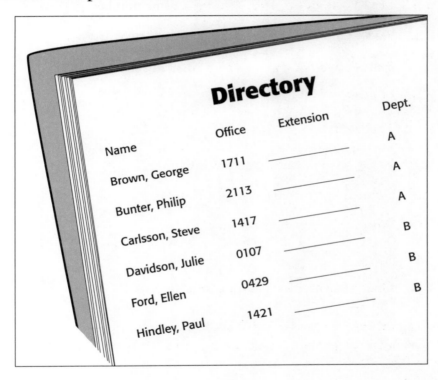

Directory

Name	Office	Extension	Dept.
Brown, George	1711	_____	A
Bunter, Philip	2113	_____	A
Carlsson, Steve	1417	_____	A
Davidson, Julie	0107	_____	B
Ford, Ellen	0429	_____	B
Hindley, Paul	1421	_____	B

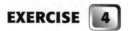

Listen to the tape and write the correct telephone numbers below.

Unit 8

The Date

EXERCISE 1

In pairs, practice saying the year. Look at these examples.

1993	19 . . . 93	nineteen ninety-three
1901	19 . . . 01	nineteen oh-one
1978	19 . . . 78	nineteen seventy-eight

EXERCISE 2

When were they born? Listen and fill in the years.

1. Marie Curie _____

2. George Washington _____

3. Mark Twain _____

4. John F. Kennedy _____

5. Elvis Presley _____

6. Susan B. Anthony _____

EXERCISE 3

Use ordinal numbers for dates. Practice saying these with a partner.

1st	the first	11th	the eleventh	21st	the twenty-first
2nd	the second	12th	the twelfth	22nd	the twenty-second
3rd	the third	13th	the thirteenth	23rd	the twenty-third
4th	the fourth	14th	the fourteenth	24th	the twenty-fourth
5th	the fifth	15th	the fifteenth	25th	the twenty-fifth
6th	the sixth	16th	the sixteenth	26th	the twenty-sixth
7th	the seventh	17th	the seventeenth	27th	the twenty-seventh
8th	the eighth	18th	the eighteenth	28th	the twenty-eighth
9th	the ninth	19th	the nineteenth	29th	the twenty-ninth
10th	the tenth	20th	the twentieth	30th	the thirtieth
				31st	the thirty-first

EXERCISE 4

Right or wrong? Listen to the tape and correct the dates below if necessary.

1. 13th _____

2. 31st _____

3. 12th _____

4. 9th _____

5. 15th _____

6. 11th _____

EXERCISE 5

Look at this calendar. Practice reading the dates.

In the United States, write the date as May 17, 1999, OR 5/17/99
Say "May seventeenth, nineteen ninety-nine."

MAY						
Sun	Mon	Tue	Wed	Thur	Fri	Sat
		1	2	3	4	5
6	7	8	9	10	11	12
13	14	15	16	17	18	19
20	21	22	23	24	25	26
27	28	29	30	31		

EXERCISE 6

Write the following dates.

1. The eighth of June, nineteen ninety-four _____

2. September sixteenth, nineteen eighty _____

3. The eleventh of October, nineteen sixty-three _____

4. July thirty-first, nineteen thirty-nine _____

5. 6/8/91 _____

6. 8/6/93 _____

7. 10/20/94 _____

8. 12/14/96 _____

EXERCISE 7

Listen to the tape and fill in the dates on Betty's list of things to do.

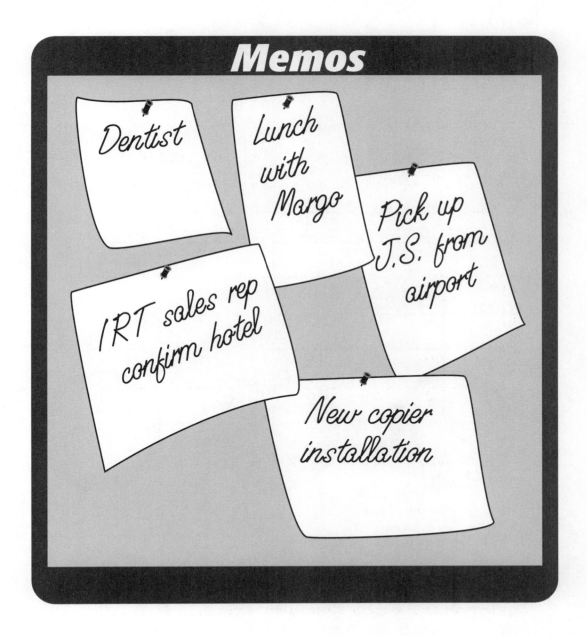

Telling Time

The Digital System.
It's ten forty-five.

EXERCISE 1

Look at these examples. Listen and repeat after the tape.

1. 6:30 in the morning
2. 2:45 in the afternoon
3. 7:00 in the evening
4. 11:20 at night

 Tip   Say A.M. before 12:00 noon and P.M. from noon until midnight.

The Classical System.
It's a quarter to eleven.

EXERCISE 2

Look at these examples. Listen and repeat after the tape.

It's 8 o'clock.   It's half past 8.   It's a quarter after 8.

It's a quarter to 8.   It's 5 after 8.   It's 10 after 8.

It's 20 after 8.

It's 25 after 8.

It's 5 to 4.

It's 10 to 4.

It's 20 to 4.

It's 25 to 4.

 Tip To find out the time, ask: "What time is it?" or if your watch or clock has stopped, "Do you have the time?"

EXERCISE 3

Change the following to classical time.

1. 12:05 A.M. _____

2. 2:25 P.M. _____

3. 10:40 A.M. _____

4. 8:55 P.M. _____

EXERCISE 4

Change the following to digital time.

1. a quarter to nine in the evening _____

2. 10 after 10 in the morning _____

3. 5 to 1 in the morning _____

4. 25 after 11 at night _____

EXERCISE  **5**

Listen to the tape. Fill in the information in this movie schedule.

METROPLEX
CINEMAS

Theater 1   **Mad Max XI** _____

_____

Theater 2   **Rocky XV** _____

_____

Theater 3   **Terminator VII** _____

_____

Theater 4   **Rambo XX** _____

_____

Theater 5   **Henry V** _____

_____

Unit 10

Spelling Clearly

EXERCISE 1

Repeat these letters after the tape.

pay [ɛɪ]	see [iː]	left [ɛ]	eye [aɪ]	go [əʊ]	blue [ʊː]	car [ɑː]
a h j k	b c d e g p t v z	f l m n s x	i y	o	q u w	r

EXERCISE 2

Practice spelling. Listen and repeat after the tape.

ROAD   LANE   STREET   WAY   CLOSE

Tip For EE, say *double E* or *E.E.*

EXERCISE 3

Practice spelling the name and address of your company with a partner. Use this International Spelling Alphabet as a guide:

A as in Amsterdam

A	Amsterdam	J	Jerusalem	S	Santiago
B	Baltimore	K	Kilogram	T	Tripoli
C	Casablanca	L	Liverpool	U	Uppsala
D	Denmark	M	Madagascar	V	Valencia
E	Edison	N	New York	W	Washington
F	Florida	O	Oslo	X	X-ray
G	Gallipoli	P	Paris	Y	Yokahama
H	Havana	Q	Québec	Z	Zürich
I	Italy	R	Rome		

EXERCISE  **4**

Invent your own spelling guide with words you know.

For example: A – apple   B – boy

A _____	J _____	S _____
B _____	K _____	T _____
C _____	L _____	U _____
D _____	M _____	V _____
E _____	N _____	W _____
F _____	O _____	X _____
G _____	P _____	Y _____
H _____	Q _____	Z _____
I _____	R _____	

EXERCISE **5**

Listen to the tape and fill in these application forms.

1.

Application

_____

Last Name   First Name

_____

Place of Birth

_____

Social Security Number

_____

Street Address

_____

City   State   Zip Code

2.

Application

Last Name   First Name

Place of Birth

Social Security Number

Street Address

City   State   Zip Code

3.

Application

Last Name   First Name

Place of Birth

Social Security Number

Street Address

City   State   Zip Code

4.

Application

_____
Last Name   First Name

_____
Place of Birth

_____
Social Security Number

_____
Street Address

_____
City   State   Zip Code

Unit 11

Taking Down an Address

EXERCISE 1

Listen to this dialogue. Repeat after the tape.

You: Could you give me the address, please?

Caller: Certainly. Are you ready?

You: Go ahead.

Caller: Quimica Colombia . . . that's Quimica . . . new word Colombia. Avenida Villa Nueva . . . 17A23/45 . . . that's Avenida . . . new word . . . Villa . . . new word . . . Nueva . . . new word . . . 17 . . . capital A . . . twenty-three . . . slash . . . 45 . . . new line . . . Bogotá . . . new line . . . Colombia.

You: Could you spell Quimica, please?

Caller: Q as in queen, U as in umbrella, I as in India, M as in mother, I as in India, C as in cat, A as in apple.

You: Thank you very much. Good-bye.

Caller: Good-bye.

 Tip Use your spelling guide to spell difficult words.

EXERCISE 2

Say these important words after the tape.

1. . period
2. - hyphen
3. — dash
4. / slash
5. ABC in capitals (or capital A, capital B, capital C)
6. abc small letters
7. PVa capital P, capital V, small a
8. new word
9. new line
10. zip code

EXERCISE 3

Look at this address. Listen to it on tape, then repeat it.

DVH Industries
1293 Division St.
Detroit, MI 48201

Now try to write it out in the same way you would say it on the phone.

_____

_____

_____

Tip When writing addresses, two-letter postal abbreviations are often used for names of states.

EXERCISE 4

Listen to the tape and write in the new addresses on these cards.

1.

> ### *Please note that*
> **Workwell Watches**
> **788 W. 51st Street**
> **Washington, DC 20003**
> ### *is moving to*
>
> _____
>
> _____
>
> ### *on January 23*

2.

The Goya Art Gallery
17 Tamworth Place
Los Angeles, CA 90025

Our new address as of March 10 will be

_____

_____

3.

CHANGE OF ADDRESS
AS OF OCTOBER 13

Pyramid Sandpapers, Inc.
224 S. Wolf Road
Birmingham, AL 35402

IS MOVING TO

_____

_____

Prepositions

EXERCISE 1

Look at the prepositions of time in the box below.

AT	BY	IN	ON	UNTIL
ten o'clock	next week	January	Monday	Wednesday
noon	the 11th	summer	the 19th of August	next year
midnight	Friday	20 minutes	New Year's Eve	the 22nd
night	June 20th	the morning	the weekend	tomorrow

EXERCISE 2

When was the accident? Fill in the time with the correct preposition.

1. It was _____ .

JUNE						
Sun	Mon	Tue	Wed	Thur	Fri	Sat
		1	2	3	4	5
6	7	8	9	10	11	12
13	14	15	16	17	18	19
20	21	22	23	24	25	26
27	28	29	30			

2. It was _____ .

3. It was _____

4. It was _____ .

5. It was _____ .

DECEMBER						
Sun	Mon.	Tue	Wed	Thur	Fri	Sat
		1	2	3	4	5
6	7	8	9	10	11	12
13	14	15	16	17	18	19
20	21	22	23	24	25	26
27	28	29	30	31		

6. It was _____.

EXERCISE 3

Study these prepositions of place.

AT	IN	ON
lunch, a conference	the U.S.	vacation
the airport, the station	California, Mexico	a business trip
the office, work	the office (inside)	a mission
home	a meeting	a special project

 Tip After a verb of movement, use *to* with all places except *home*. He drives *to* the office. I flew *to* Nashville. They're going *to* the café. We went home.

EXERCISE 4

Where's Mr. Hernandez? Fill in the preposition.

1. He's _____ work.

2. He's _____ lunch.

3. He's _____ a business trip.

4. He's _____ vacation.

5. He's _____ a meeting.

6. He's _____ New York.

EXERCISE 5

Fill in the blanks with a preposition.

1. Please ask Mr. Smith to meet me _____ Union Station

   _____ May 3rd _____ 11:00.

2. Terry is _____ Mexico _____ a

   business trip _____ the silver factory this week.

3. Our phone rings more _____ the morning than

   _____ the afternoon and never

   _____ the evening.

4. I'll be _____ my office or _____

   the conference _____ Wednesday when you arrive.

5. The company will be closed _____ August and

   _____ Christmas Day.

6. I'm coming _____ Tokyo _____

   Friday and staying _____ Tuesday.

7. Please finish this project _____ the end of the month.

8. Mrs. Brown's secretary is going _____ the bank before

   she goes _____ home.

EXERCISE 6

Fill in the prepositions.

1. _____ night
   work
   a conference

2. _____ Wednesday
   the 1st of June
   vacation

3. _____ the morning
   Australia
   February

4. _____ 3 o'clock
   home
   noon

Unit 13

Basic Language Review

This Unit reviews the most important language in Units 1–12.

EXERCISE [1]

Fill in one word in each blank in these conversations.

1. You: Rapide Communications. Good morning.

    Caller: Good morning. Could I speak to Mr. Davidson,

    _____?

    You: _____. _____ I have

    your name, _____?

    Caller: Mark Schwarz from Dallas.

    You: _____ one moment, Mr. Schwarz.

2. You: Ms. Carleton's secretary. How can I help you?

    Caller: I'd like to speak to Ms. Carleton, please.

    You: _____. Ms. Carleton is

    _____ vacation this week.

    _____ you like to leave a

    _____?

    Caller: Yes, could you ask her to call me when she gets back?

    My name is Sussman.

    You: Could you _____ that,

    _____?

    Caller: It's S–U– _____ S–M–A–N.

    You: Thank you, Mr. Sussman. I'll make sure she gets the message.

3.   You: Extension 230.

   Caller: Oh, I'm sorry. I asked for extension 320.

   You: Hold _____, please. I'll

   _____ you back to the

   _____.

EXERCISE 2

Match the phrase on the left with the phrase on the right that has the same meaning.

_____ 1. Hold on.   a. Good-bye

_____ 2. I'd like to . . .   b. Pardon?

_____ 3. I'll connect you.   c. Connect

_____ 4. Yes.   d. Call again.

_____ 5. I'm sorry . . .   e. Who's calling?

_____ 6. So long.   f. Can I . . .

_____ 7. Sorry?   g. Please wait.

_____ 8. Call back.   h. I'm afraid . . .

_____ 9. Who's speaking?   i. I'll put you through.

_____ 10. Put through   j. Certainly.

EXERCISE 3

Fill in the blanks below with the correct words.

When you make an international call, first you dial the

_____ _____, then you dial the

_____ _____, then you dial

the number.

Fill in the blanks in these recorded messages.

1. Thank you for _____ Goodkin, Smith, and Associates.

   I'm sorry. There's _____ here to answer your call. If

   you _____ your name and telephone number after the

   _____, we'll _____ you back as

   _____ as we can.

2. CPA Incorporated. All lines are currently busy. Please remain on the

   _____ and your call will be answered shortly.

3. Mediterranean Tours. Our office is now _____ for the

   day. Our office hours are from 9:30 _____ until 5:30

   _____. If you _____ like us to call

   you _____, please leave your name and number after

   the tone.

EXERCISE 5

Put this conversation in the correct order.

_____ a. I'm sorry, but she's in a meeting. Could I take a message?

_____ b. Certainly. I'll let her know.

_____ c. Good-bye.

_____ d. Music International. Good afternoon.

_____ e. Certainly. Thank you for calling.

_____ f. Good afternoon. May I speak to Ms. Bellamy, please? This is her travel agent.

_____ g. Could you also tell her I'll put her tickets in the mail today?

_____ h. Yes, of course. Could you tell Ms. Bellamy her flight to Los Angeles on the 13th has been changed? The departure time is now 9:30 A.M., not 10:30 A.M.

EXERCISE  6

Look at this address. Then fill in the blanks below.

> New Style Wool Sweaters
> Dept. KK5/BAF
> 205 Bradford Road
> Omaha, NE 61801

New Style Wool Sweaters—that's four words: New Style Wool Sweaters,

New _____: Department KK5/BAF—that's

_____ K _____ K 5

_____ _____ B

_____ A _____ F. New

_____: two oh five Bradford Road. New

_____: Omaha—I'll _____ that:

O–M–A–H–A—Nebraska. The _____ is 61801.

EXERCISE 7

Here are some of the most important phrases from Units 1–12. Only the first part is given. Complete the phrases.

1. Can I speak to Mr. Martin, _____?

2. Who's _____?

3. One _____.

4. I'll _____ you.

5. May I take a _____?

6. Could you tell her I _____?

7. I'm sorry. There's nobody by _____.

8. I'm very sorry. I must have the _____.

9. Please confirm by _____.

10. I'm sorry. The connection is very _____.

EXERCISE 8

Fill in a preposition in each of the following phrases.

1. _____ the morning

2. _____ the afternoon

3. _____ the evening

4. _____ night

5. _____ the phone

6. _____ the line

7. _____ vacation

8. _____ a meeting

9. _____ home

10. _____ another line

11. _____ the tone

12. _____ 3 o'clock

13. _____ Thursday

14. _____ 9:00 A.M.

_____ 6:00 P.M.

15. _____ May 1

16. _____ a business trip

17. _____ Friday afternoon

18. _____ lunch

19. _____ work

20. the area code _____
Baltimore

Unit 14a

Listening Practice

EXERCISE

Write the numbers you hear on the tape.

1. _____ 2. _____ 3. _____

4. _____ 5. _____

EXERCISE

Write the letters you hear.

1. _____ 2. _____ 3. _____

4. _____ 5. _____

EXERCISE

Write the flight numbers you hear.

1. _____ 2. _____ 3. _____

4. _____ 5. _____

EXERCISE

Write the letters you hear.

1. _____ 2. _____ 3. _____

4. _____ 5. _____

📞 **PHONE PLAY**   **Student A**

Call Student B. Ask to speak to Mr. Smith.

Getting the Message

Listen to the message on the tape. Make a note of the important information.

 Tip Make sure you write down the important details. You don't need to write down every word.

IMPORTANT MESSAGE

To _____

Date_____ Time _____ A.M. / P.M.

From _____

Of _____

Phone _____
   Area Code   Number   Time to Call

☐ Fax   _____
   Area Code   Number   Time to Call

☐ Mobile _____
   Area Code   Number   Time to Call

Message _____

_____

_____

_____

_____

_____

_____

_____

 PHONE PLAY   **Student B**

Student A will call you. Ask his name. Connect him to Mr. Smith.

Unit 15a

Listening Practice

EXERCISE 1

Write the numbers you hear on the tape.

1. _____ 2. _____ 3. _____

4. _____ 5. _____

EXERCISE 2

Circle the letter you hear.

1. B G D V   2. E P C T   3. I Q U Y

4. X F M S   5. Z N F X

EXERCISE 3

Write the year you hear.

1. _____ 2. _____ 3. _____

4. _____ 5. _____

EXERCISE 4

Listen carefully. Write down exactly what you hear.

1. _____ 2. _____ 3. _____

📞 **PHONE PLAY**   **Student A**

Call Student B. Ask to speak to Mr. Wilson.

Unit 15b

Getting the Message

Listen to the message on the tape. Make a note of the important information.

 Tip Remember to write down only the important details.

```
┌─────────────────────────────────────────────────────┐
│              ╭─────────────────────────╮             │
│              │   IMPORTANT MESSAGE      │             │
│              ╰─────────────────────────╯             │
│                                                       │
│   To _____  │
│                                            A.M.       │
│   Date_____ Time_____ P.M.     │
│                                                       │
│   From _____   │
│   Of _____   │
│   Phone _____   │
│              Area Code    Number        Time to Call  │
│                                                       │
│   ☐ Fax   _____   │
│              Area Code    Number        Time to Call  │
│                                                       │
│   ☐ Mobile _____   │
│              Area Code    Number        Time to Call  │
│                                                       │
│   Message _____   │
│   _____   │
│   _____   │
│   _____   │
│   _____   │
│   _____   │
│   _____   │
│   _____   │
│                                                       │
└─────────────────────────────────────────────────────┘
```

 PHONE PLAY **Student B**

Student A will call you. Ask for his name.
Mr. Wilson is out until 4 o'clock.

Unit 16a

Listening Practice

EXERCISE 1

Write the letters you hear on the tape.

1. _____   2. _____   3. _____

4. _____   5. _____

EXERCISE 2

Write the telephone numbers you hear.

1. _____   2. _____   3. _____

4. _____   5. _____

EXERCISE 3

Fill in the missing letters you hear.

1. k _____ d e   2. b _____ l x   3. _____ o g f

4. x z b _____   5. p r _____ i

EXERCISE 4

Circle the number you hear.

1. 80   18   2. 70   17   3. 16   60

4. 15   50   5. 30   13

PHONE PLAY   **Student A**

Call Student B. Give your name. Ask to speak to Mrs. Taylor. You have a meeting at 3:00.

Getting the Message

Listen to the message on the tape. Make a note of the important information.

IMPORTANT MESSAGE

To _____

Date_____ Time _____ A.M. / P.M.

From _____

Of _____

Phone_____
      Area Code   Number   Time to Call

☐ Fax _____
      Area Code   Number   Time to Call

☐ Mobile _____
      Area Code   Number   Time to Call

Message _____
_____
_____
_____
_____
_____
_____
_____

 PHONE PLAY   **Student B**

You are Mrs. Taylor's assistant. Mrs. Taylor is at lunch. She is coming back at 3:00.

Unit 17a

Listening Practice

EXERCISE 1

Write the phone numbers you hear on the tape.

1. _____ 2. _____ 3. _____

4. _____ 5. _____

EXERCISE 2

Write the month and year you hear.

1. _____ 2. _____ 3. _____

4. _____ 5. _____

EXERCISE 3

Write the letters you hear.

1. _____ 2. _____ 3. _____

4. _____ 5. _____

EXERCISE 4

Write the times you hear.

1. _____ 2. _____ 3. _____

4. _____ 5. _____

 PHONE PLAY   **Student A**

Call Student B. Your name is Mr. Bradburn. You want to confirm your
appointment tomorrow with Miss Wells.

Getting the Message

Listen to the message on the tape. Make a note of the important information.

```
┌─────────────────────────────────────────────────┐
│         ╭─────────────────────────╮              │
│         │    IMPORTANT MESSAGE    │              │
│         ╰─────────────────────────╯              │
│                                                   │
│   To _____         │
│                                          A.M.     │
│   Date_____ Time_____ P.M.          │
│                                                   │
│   From _____         │
│   Of _____         │
│   Phone_____          │
│         Area Code   Number      Time to Call      │
│                                                   │
│   ☐ Fax  _____          │
│         Area Code   Number      Time to Call      │
│                                                   │
│   ☐ Mobile _____          │
│         Area Code   Number      Time to Call      │
│                                                   │
│   Message _____          │
│   _____          │
│   _____          │
│   _____          │
│   _____          │
│   _____          │
│   _____          │
│   _____          │
│   _____          │
└─────────────────────────────────────────────────┘
```

📞 **PHONE PLAY**   **Student B**

You are Miss Wells's colleague. Miss Wells is ill. Her appointments are canceled this week.

Unit 18a

Listening Practice

EXERCISE 1

Write the dates you hear on the tape.

1. _____ 2. _____ 3. _____

4. _____ 5. _____

EXERCISE 2

Write the times you hear.

1. _____ 2. _____ 3. _____

4. _____ 5. _____

EXERCISE 3

Write the telephone numbers you hear.

1. _____ 2. _____ 3. _____

4. _____ 5. _____

EXERCISE 4

Listen to the phrases on the tape. Underline the word or syllable that is stressed in each sentence. Then practice saying them yourself.

1. One moment, please.   2. Who's calling, please?

3. May I help you?   4. He's in a meeting.

📞 PHONE PLAY   Student A

Call Student B. You are Mr. Kostalas. Ask for Mr. Dioso. You want to meet him tomorrow. You are busy on Thursday. Today is Tuesday.

Getting the Message

Listen to the message on the tape. Make a note of the important information.

```
┌─────────────────────────────────────────────────┐
│                                                   │
│          ╭─────────────────────────╮              │
│          │   IMPORTANT MESSAGE     │              │
│          ╰─────────────────────────╯              │
│                                                   │
│   To _____          │
│                                         A.M.       │
│   Date_____  Time _____   P.M.        │
│                                                   │
│   From _____          │
│   Of _____          │
│   Phone _____          │
│           Area Code    Number      Time to Call    │
│                                                   │
│   □ Fax    _____          │
│           Area Code    Number      Time to Call    │
│                                                   │
│   □ Mobile _____          │
│           Area Code    Number      Time to Call    │
│                                                   │
│   Message _____          │
│   _____          │
│   _____          │
│   _____          │
│   _____          │
│   _____          │
│   _____          │
│   _____          │
│                                                   │
└─────────────────────────────────────────────────┘
```

PHONE PLAY   Student B

Call Mr. Dioso. You have a meeting tomorrow, but you are free on Thursday and Friday. Today is Tuesday.

Unit 19a

Listening Practice

EXERCISE

Write the telephone numbers you hear on the tape.

1. _____ 2. _____ 3. _____

4. _____ 5. _____

EXERCISE

Circle the letters you hear.

1. BI BA BE BY   2. HY HI AE AI   3. AM EM IM OM

4. JE GE JI GI   5. BB BV VB VV

EXERCISE

Write the times you hear.

1. _____ 2. _____ 3. _____

4. _____ 5. _____

EXERCISE

Listen carefully. Write down exactly what you hear.

1. _____ 2. _____ 3. _____

4. _____ 5. _____

 PHONE PLAY   **Student A**

Call the Executive Travel Service. You want to book a flight from Chicago
to Los Angeles on Wednesday the 12th at 8:00 A.M. for your boss.

Getting the Message

Listen to the message on the tape. Make a note of the important information.

┌───┐

IMPORTANT MESSAGE

To _____

Date _____ Time _____ A.M. / P.M.

From _____

Of _____

Phone _____
       Area Code   Number   Time to Call

☐ Fax _____
       Area Code   Number   Time to Call

☐ Mobile _____
       Area Code   Number   Time to Call

Message _____
_____
_____
_____
_____
_____
_____
_____
_____

└───┘

☎ **PHONE PLAY**   **Student B**

You work for the Executive Travel Service. (Give the name of your company when you answer.) The morning flights from Chicago to Los Angeles leave at 6:00 A.M., 7:00 A.M., and 9:00 A.M. Flights from Milwaukee to Los Angeles leave at 8:00 A.M. and 10:00 A.M.

Unit 20a

Listening Practice

EXERCISE 1

Write the phone numbers you hear on the tape.

1. _____   2. _____   3. _____

4. _____   5. _____

EXERCISE 2

Write the dates you hear.

1. _____   2. _____   3. _____

4. _____   5. _____

EXERCISE 3

Circle the number you hear.

1. 101 110 111   2. 218 280 880   3. 333 303 323

4. 616 660 666   5. 719 790 729

EXERCISE 4

Write the address you hear.

_____

_____

_____

 PHONE PLAY   **Student A**

You are Mr. Lewis of American Motors, Incorporated. Call Mr. Takenashe.
You can't go to the sales meeting on June 5 in Tokyo. You won't be able to
meet him in July because you will be on vacation.

Getting the Message

Listen to the message on the tape. Make a note of the important information.

IMPORTANT MESSAGE

To _____

Date_____ Time_____ A.M.
P.M.

From _____

Of _____

Phone_____
        Area Code   Number   Time to Call

☐ Fax   _____
        Area Code   Number   Time to Call

☐ Mobile _____
        Area Code   Number   Time to Call

Message _____

_____

_____

_____

_____

_____

_____

_____

📞 **PHONE PLAY**   **Student B**

You are Mr. Takenashe's colleague. Mr. Takenashe is in the hospital. The meeting is postponed until July 10.

Unit 21a

Listening Practice

EXERCISE 1

Write the names of the cities you hear on the tape.

1. _____   2. _____   3. _____

4. _____   5. _____

EXERCISE 2

Write the times you hear.

1. _____   2. _____   3. _____

4. _____   5. _____

EXERCISE 3

Write the dates you hear.

1. _____   2. _____   3. _____

4. _____   5. _____

EXERCISE 4

Circle the group of letters you hear.

1. WVU   VWY   YWV   UVW   2. HAE   EIH   HAI   IEA

3. GYJ   JGJ   YJG   IYG   4. VVB   DBV   BBB   BVV

PHONE PLAY   Student A

Call the New Yorker Hotel. You need a double room for 3 nights from
May 9 to May 12. You have a baby. Ask for prices and book the room.

Unit 21b

Getting the Message

Listen to the message on the tape. Make a note of the important information.

IMPORTANT MESSAGE

To _____

Date_____ Time _____ A.M. / P.M.

From _____

Of _____

Phone _____
      Area Code   Number   Time to Call

☐ Fax _____
      Area Code   Number   Time to Call

☐ Mobile _____
      Area Code   Number   Time to Call

Message _____

_____

_____

_____

_____

_____

_____

_____

📞 **PHONE PLAY**   **Student B**

You are the receptionist at the New Yorker Hotel. A single room costs $110 per night; a double room costs $150. Dogs and children are free. Ask for Student A's name.

58   Basic Telephone Training

Unit 22a

Listening Practice

EXERCISE

Write the dates you hear on the tape.

1._____   2._____   3._____

4._____   5._____

EXERCISE

Write the letters you hear.

1._____   2._____   3._____

4._____   5._____

EXERCISE

Circle the time you hear.

1. 11:15 7:15   2. 8:40 8:14   3. 1:50 2:10

4. 3:15 3:50   5. 5:15 4:45

EXERCISE

Write the address you hear.

_____

_____

_____

_____

  PHONE PLAY   **Student A**

You work for the Office Paper Shop. Phone Mr. Henderson at Paper Suppliers,
Incorporated to place an urgent order for 8,000 white window envelopes.

Getting the Message

Listen to the message on the tape. Make a note of the important information.

```
┌─────────────────────────────────────────────┐
│                                               │
│        ╭───────────────────────────╮          │
│        │    IMPORTANT MESSAGE      │          │
│        ╰───────────────────────────╯          │
│                                               │
│   To _____        │
│                                      A.M.     │
│   Date_____ Time _____ P.M.        │
│                                               │
│   From _____        │
│   Of _____        │
│   Phone _____        │
│         Area Code   Number      Time to Call  │
│                                               │
│   ☐ Fax    _____          │
│         Area Code   Number      Time to Call  │
│                                               │
│   ☐ Mobile _____          │
│         Area Code   Number      Time to Call  │
│                                               │
│   Message _____         │
│   _____         │
│   _____         │
│   _____         │
│   _____         │
│   _____         │
│   _____         │
│   _____         │
│                                               │
└─────────────────────────────────────────────┘
```

📞 **PHONE PLAY**   **Student B**

You work for Paper Suppliers, Incorporated. You are Mr. Henderson's colleague. He is on vacation for 2 weeks. You sell envelopes. On orders under 10,000, there is no discount. On orders over 10,000, you give a 10% discount.

Unit 23a

Listening Practice

EXERCISE 1

Write the phone numbers you hear on the tape.

1. _____ 2. _____ 3. _____

4. _____ 5. _____

EXERCISE 2

Write the names of the countries you hear.

1. _____ 2. _____ 3. _____

4. _____ 5. _____

EXERCISE 3

Circle the date you hear.

1. 9/3/90   3/9/91   2. 6/17/89   7/17/89   3. 10/14/92   10/4/92

4. 3/21/73   3/31/73   5. 8/20/84   12/31/99

EXERCISE 4

Write the address you hear.

_____

_____

_____

_____

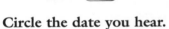 **PHONE PLAY**   **Student A**

Call Jeff Morris. Give your name. You can't go to the restaurant with him today. You want to change the lunch to tomorrow.

Getting the Message

Listen to the message on the tape. Make a note of the important information.

IMPORTANT MESSAGE

To _____

Date _____ Time _____ A.M.
P.M.

From _____

Of _____

Phone _____
       Area Code   Number   Time to Call

☐ Fax _____
       Area Code   Number   Time to Call

☐ Mobile _____
       Area Code   Number   Time to Call

Message _____

_____

_____

_____

_____

_____

_____

_____

_____

 PHONE PLAY   **Student B**

You are Jeff Morris's secretary. Mr. Morris is out all morning. You don't know where he is. He's going directly to the Gourmand Restaurant at 12:30.

Unit 24a

Listening Practice

EXERCISE 1

Write the times you hear on the tape.

1. _____ 2. _____ 3. _____

4. _____ 5. _____

EXERCISE 2

Write the names of the airports you hear.

1. _____ 2. _____ 3. _____

4. _____ 5. _____

EXERCISE 3

Listen to the phrases on the tape. Underline the word or syllable that is stressed in each sentence. Then practice saying them yourself.

1. He's out of town this week.   2. Can he call you back at five o'clock?

3. The meeting's canceled.   4. What's your address, please?

EXERCISE 4

Write the special dates you hear. What are their names?

1. _____ 2. _____ 3. _____

4. _____ 5. _____

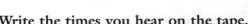 **PHONE PLAY**   **Student A**

Call Double Peaks Travel. You are Mr. Todd. Change your flight from New York to Seattle from October 21 to October 22. You have a coach class ticket.

Getting the Message

Listen to the message on the tape. Make a note of the important information.

```
┌─────────────────────────────────────────────────────┐
│         ╭───────────────────────────╮                │
│         │    IMPORTANT MESSAGE      │                │
│         ╰───────────────────────────╯                │
│                                                       │
│  To _____            │
│                                          A.M.         │
│  Date_____  Time_____ P.M.             │
│                                                       │
│  From _____            │
│  Of _____            │
│  Phone_____             │
│         Area Code    Number         Time to Call      │
│                                                       │
│  ☐ Fax  _____             │
│         Area Code    Number         Time to Call      │
│                                                       │
│  ☐ Mobile _____             │
│           Area Code  Number         Time to Call      │
│                                                       │
│  Message _____            │
│  _____             │
│  _____             │
│  _____             │
│  _____             │
│  _____             │
│  _____             │
│  _____             │
│  _____             │
└─────────────────────────────────────────────────────┘
```

 PHONE PLAY   **Student B**

You work at Double Peaks Travel. Coach class is full on all flights from New York to Seattle from October 22 to October 25. Suggest business class on the 22nd. (There is a seat in coach on the 21st but it is on the late flight, leaving at 11:00 P.M.)

Unit 25a

Listening Practice

EXERCISE 1

Write down the first names you hear on the tape.

1. _____ 2. _____ 3. _____

4. _____ 5. _____

EXERCISE 2

Write the phone numbers you hear.

1. _____ 2. _____ 3. _____

4. _____ 5. _____

EXERCISE 3

Write the times you hear.

1. _____ 2. _____ 3. _____

4. _____ 5. _____

EXERCISE 4

Write the Canadian address you hear. Listen carefully.

_____

_____

_____

_____

 PHONE PLAY   **Student A**

Call FASG Chemicals. Your name is George Drake. You work for Agri Pro.
Ask for the Technical Manager of FASG. You want some information on
new phosphate products.

Getting the Message

Listen to the message on the tape. Make a note of the important information.

IMPORTANT MESSAGE

To _____

Date_____ Time _____ A.M.
P.M.

From _____

Of _____

Phone_____
        Area Code   Number   Time to Call

☐ Fax   _____
        Area Code   Number   Time to Call

☐ Mobile _____
        Area Code   Number   Time to Call

Message _____

_____

_____

_____

_____

_____

_____

_____

📞 PHONE PLAY   Student B

You work for FASG Chemicals. The Technical Manager is in South America this week. Suggest a presentation on new phosphates developments at FASG. Decide on a date and time. Ask for Student A's name and the name of his company.

Unit 26a

Listening Practice

EXERCISE

Write the names of the cities you hear on the tape.

1. _____ 2. _____ 3. _____

4. _____ 5. _____

EXERCISE 2

Write the dates you hear.

1. _____ 2. _____ 3. _____

4. _____ 5. _____

EXERCISE

Circle the time you hear.

1. 1:30   2:30   2. 2:00 P.M.   2:00 A.M.   3. 10:15   9:45

4. 2:15   1:45   5. 9:30   7:30

EXERCISE

Write the address you hear.

_____

_____

_____

_____

 PHONE PLAY   **Student A**

You want to buy a Cox Word Processor for your office. Call Cox Office
Machines and ask for the Sales Department. Ask about price, delivery, and
discounts.

Unit 26b

Getting the Message

Listen to the message on the tape. Make a note of the important information.

IMPORTANT MESSAGE

To _____

Date_____ Time_____ A.M.
                                                P.M.

From _____

Of _____

Phone_____
        Area Code   Number   Time to Call

☐ Fax _____
        Area Code   Number   Time to Call

☐ Mobile _____
        Area Code   Number   Time to Call

Message _____

_____

_____

_____

_____

_____

_____

_____

PHONE PLAY   **Student B**

You work for Cox Office Machines. Invite Student A for a demonstration.
Decide on a date and time. Take his name and the name of his company.

Unit 27a

Listening Practice

EXERCISE 1

Write the numbers you hear on the tape.

1. _____ 2. _____ 3. _____

4. _____ 5. _____

EXERCISE 2

Write the surnames you hear.

1. _____ 2. _____ 3. _____

4. _____ 5. _____

EXERCISE 3

Circle the dates you hear.

1. 8/30/92 8/31/92   2. May 30   May 13   3. March 6   March 16

4. April 26   April 25   5. March 31   May 31

EXERCISE 4

Listen to the phrases on the tape. Underline the word or syllable that is stressed in each sentence. Then practice saying them yourself.

1. I'll put you through.   2. I'd like to speak to Mr. Imari, please.

3. I'm afraid he's out all afternoon.   4. What time will he be available?

PHONE PLAY   Student A

Call Mrs. Cupp at Peer Pottery. You have just received order no. BC/56. You ordered 24 place settings, but only 18 were delivered. There are 24 on the invoice.

Getting the Message

Listen to the message on the tape. Make a note of the important information.

IMPORTANT MESSAGE

To _____

Date _____ Time _____ A.M.
                                                P.M.

From _____

Of _____

Phone _____
       Area Code   Number   Time to Call

☐ Fax _____
       Area Code   Number   Time to Call

☐ Mobile _____
       Area Code   Number   Time to Call

Message _____

_____

_____

_____

_____

_____

_____

_____

 **PHONE PLAY**   **Student B**

You are Mrs. Cupp's secretary at Peer Pottery. Mrs. Cupp is out of the country this week. Listen to Student A's problem and suggest a solution (change invoice, complete order . . .).

Unit 28a

Listening Practice

EXERCISE 1

Circle the number you hear on the tape.

1. 2,894   2,844
2. 26,808   26,008
3. 17,659   70,659
4. 13,000   30,000
5. 6,142   6,642

EXERCISE 2

Write the dates you hear.

1. _____
2. _____
3. _____
4. _____
5. _____

EXERCISE 3

Write the times you hear.

1. _____
2. _____
3. _____
4. _____
5. _____

EXERCISE 4

Write the Mexican address you hear.

_____

_____

_____

_____

PHONE PLAY   Student A

You are Mr. Biggs, owner of the Perfume Shop. Call Rucci Beauty Products
and ask for Mr. Rucci. You can't pay invoice no. 66329 of $1,550 right
away. Invent a good reason!

Unit 28b

Getting the Message

Listen to the message on the tape. Make a note of the important information.

```
┌─────────────────────────────────────────────┐
│         ╭────────────────────────╮            │
│         │   IMPORTANT MESSAGE    │            │
│         ╰────────────────────────╯            │
│                                                │
│  To _____   │
│                                         A.M.   │
│  Date_____  Time _____   P.M.    │
│                                                │
│  From _____  │
│  Of _____  │
│  Phone_____  │
│         Area Code    Number        Time to Call│
│                                                │
│  ☐ Fax   _____   │
│          Area Code   Number        Time to Call│
│                                                │
│  ☐ Mobile _____   │
│           Area Code  Number        Time to Call│
│                                                │
│  Message _____   │
│  _____  │
│  _____  │
│  _____  │
│  _____  │
│  _____  │
│  _____  │
│  _____  │
│  _____  │
└─────────────────────────────────────────────┘
```

☎ **PHONE PLAY**   **Student B**

You work for Rucci Beauty Products. Mr. Rucci is busy and can't be disturbed. Try to help Student A (who is always a bad customer).

Answer Key

This key contains the answers to all the exercises and the full text of all recorded material not printed in the student units. In exercises where there is more than one answer, suggested answers are given.

Unit 1

EXERCISE 2

1. d   2. a   3. e   4. c   5. b

EXERCISE 4

Script:

1.   You: <u>Good morning</u>. Interface. May I help you?

      Caller: Hello. <u>May</u> I speak to Mr. Stevenson, please?

      You: <u>One</u> moment, please. I'm <u>connecting you</u>.

2.   You: <u>Good afternoon</u>. PLC International.

      Caller: <u>I'd like to</u> speak to Mr. Davies, please.

      You: Who's <u>calling</u>, please?

      Caller: <u>This is</u> Charles Williamson of Micro Logics.

      You: <u>One moment</u>, please. I'll <u>connect you</u>.

EXERCISE 5

1. Good morning. Belfry Consultants.
2. May I speak to Mr. Brown, please?
3. May I have your name, please? (Who's calling?)
4. Brian Howard from Jason's.
5. One moment, Mr. Howard.
6. I'll connect you.

EXERCISE 6

1. Australia 61
2. India 91
3. Brazil 55
4. Mexico 52
5. Los Angeles (213)
6. Washington, D.C. (202)
7. Chicago (312), (773)
8. Atlanta (404), (678)

Unit 2

EXERCISE 2

1. c   2. h   3. f   4. a   5. i   6. e   7. b   8. d   9. g

EXERCISE 3

Script:

1.   You: I'm <u>afraid</u> Mr. Jones is <u>in a meeting</u>.

      Caller: Oh dear! <u>When</u> will he be <u>available</u>?

      You: At about <u>4:00</u>.

      Caller: Well, could you <u>take a message</u>, please?

2.   You: Hello. I'm <u>sorry</u>, but Gloria is <u>on another line</u>. May I <u>help you</u>?

    Caller: No, that's all right. Could you just <u>tell her I called</u>.

EXERCISE 4

Suggested answers:

    You: Good morning. José Vidal speaking.

  Caller: I'd like to speak to Mrs. Rossi, please.

    You: I'm sorry, but Mrs. Rossi is out at the moment. Can you call back later?

  Caller: What time will she be back?

    You: In about 20 minutes.

  Caller: Thank you very much.

    You: You're welcome. Good-bye.

EXERCISE 5

Script:

1. He won't be back until <u>Thursday</u> morning.
2. We open again on <u>Tuesday</u> morning at 9:00.
3. We will be closed from <u>Monday</u> the 16th until <u>Wednesday</u> the 18th.
4. The best time to call is before lunch on <u>Fridays</u> or after 5:00 P.M. on <u>Mondays</u>.

EXERCISE 6

1. 16th	**2.** 17th	**3.** 15th	**4.** 23rd
5. 24th	**6.** 9th	**7.** 31st	

Unit 3

EXERCISE 2

1. a   **2.** c   **3.** e   **4.** b   **5.** d

EXERCISE 3

Suggested answers:

  Caller: Is this Tell Brothers?

    You: No, this is <u>LTP, Incorporated</u>.

  Caller: I'd like to speak to Miss Van Hertzen, please.

    You: I'm sorry. There's <u>no one here by that name</u>.

  Caller: Is this 489-9929?

    You: No, <u>this is 489-9299</u>.

EXERCISE 4

Script:

    You: Good afternoon. Susan McQueen speaking.

  Caller: Is <u>this</u> extension 584?

    You: No, this is extension 554. I'll <u>reconnect</u> you to the switchboard.

  Caller: Thanks for your help.

    You: That's all right. Good-bye.

EXERCISE 5

Suggested answers:

1. Good afternoon. May I speak to Patricia Smith, please?

   <u>I'm sorry. There's nobody here by that name. My name's Dorothy Smith.</u>

2. Is this 992-4897?

   <u>I'm afraid you've got the wrong number. This is 992-4097.</u>

3. Good morning. I'd like to speak to Mr. Thomson, please.

   <u>I'm sorry. There's no Mr. Thomson here.</u>

EXERCISE 6

1. a   2. h   3. g   4. b   5. e   6. d   7. c   8. f

Unit 4

EXERCISE 3

This is Paul Downs speaking.

<u>Pardon?</u>

Paul Downs speaking.

<u>I'm sorry,</u> but the connection is very bad.

Paul Downs.

Could you <u>spell</u> that, <u>please?</u>

P–A–U–L D–O–W–N–S.

Could you <u>repeat</u> that, please?

P–A–U–L D–O–W–N–S.

<u>Sorry,</u> but I <u>still</u> don't understand.

P–A–U—

Ah, good afternoon, Mr. Downs. How are you?

EXERCISE 4

1. pardon   2. slowly   3. understand   4. still   5. up

6. repeat   7. English   8. connection   9. confirm

Unit 5

EXERCISE 2

Suggested answers: you have reached, thank you for calling, our office is currently closed, leave your name, return your call, apologize for the delay, call you back, if you have an urgent message.

EXERCISE 3

Suggested answers:

1. This is _____. I'm sorry. I'm not available at the moment. Please call back tomorrow.

2. I'm sorry, but our office is closed for the day. We are open from _____ to _____, Monday to Friday. Please call back tomorrow.

3. The office is closed this afternoon. Please call again tomorrow after 9:00 A.M. Thank you for calling.

EXERCISE 4

Script:
1. This is <u>LTP</u>, Incorporated. Please <u>hold</u>. We're sorry to <u>keep you waiting.</u>
2. This is Henry Barber's office. I'm <u>not available</u> right now, but if you leave me <u>your name</u> and your phone number, I'll <u>call you back</u> when I return. Please speak <u>after the beep.</u>

Unit 6

EXERCISE 3

1. fifty-one
2. eight hundred twelve
3. four thousand, seven hundred thirty-nine
4. two hundred four thousand, one hundred ten

EXERCISE 4

1. 28,914
2. 704
3. 2,351
4. 634,405

EXERCISE 5

Across: 1. 232   3. 3,084   5. 94   6. 40,968
       10. 45,089   11. 23   13. 2,690   14. 513

Down: 1. 219,914   2. 27   3. 3,102   4. 8,765
      7. 824,363   8. 7,516   9. 4,860   12. 75

Unit 7

EXERCISE 2

1. (217) 555-9651
2. (601) 012-7832
3. (305) 012-5733
4. (414) 551-0884

EXERCISE 3

1. Brown: extension 476
2. Bunter: extension 122
3. Carlsson: extension 880
4. Davidson: extension 326
5. Ford: extension 115
6. Hindley: extension 904

EXERCISE 4

1. Frankfurt 69 80 455
2. London 1 56 48 66
3. Mexico City 52 84 550
4. Seoul 2 514 67 00
5. Tokyo 1 51 88 44
6. Toronto 0 356 081

Unit 8

EXERCISE 2

Script:
1. Curie 1867
2. Washington 1732
3. Twain 1835
4. Kennedy 1917
5. Presley 1935
6. Anthony 1820

EXERCISE 4

Script
1. 30th (wrong)
2. 31st (correct)
3. 10th (wrong)
4. 19th (wrong)
5. 5th (wrong)
6. 11th (correct)

EXERCISE 6

1. 6/8/94   **2.** 9/16/80   **3.** 10/11/63   **4.** 7/31/39

5. June eighth, nineteen ninety-one

6. the sixth of August, nineteen ninety-three

7. the twentieth of October, nineteen ninety-four

8. December fourteenth, nineteen ninety-six

EXERCISE 7

Script:

Now, I mustn't forget to pick up John Sanderson from the airport on the 19th. I'm having lunch with Margo on the 22nd and I have to confirm the IRT Sales Representative's hotel on the 24th. Oh yes, they're coming to install the new copier on the 20th and I must remember my appointment on the 21st.

Unit 9

EXERCISE 3

1. five after twelve   **2.** twenty-five after two

3. twenty to eleven   **4.** five to nine

EXERCISE 4

1. 8:45 P.M.   **2.** 10:10 A.M.   **3.** 12:55 A.M.   **4.** 11:25 P.M.

EXERCISE 5

Script:

Welcome to the Metroplex Cinemas. Here are the times of our movies this week:

In Theater 1 you can see *Mad Max 11*, showing at 2:00, 4:35, 7:25, and 10:00.

In Theater 2 *Rocky 15* is showing at 1:30, 4:15, 7:00, and 9:45.

In Theater 3 *Terminator 7* is showing at 1:50, 4:30, 7:10, and 8:50.

In Theater 4 *Rambo 20* is showing at 1:35, 4:15, 6:55, and 8:35.

And finally, in Theater 5 *Henry the Fifth* is showing at 1:15, 4:35, and 8:55.

Unit 10

EXERCISE 4

Suggested answers: Apple, Book, Cat, Dog, Elephant, France, Germany, Hello, India, Japan, King, Lion, McDonald's, North, Orange, Peter, Queen, Rat, Snow, Think, Under, Victory, William, X-ray, Yes, Zebra.

EXERCISE 5

1. Last Name: Hackworth **First Name:** Larry

Place of birth: Phoenix, Arizona, U.S.A.

Social Security Number: 443-17-9246

Street Address: 1232 Jefferson Avenue

City, State, Zip Code: Santa Fe, NM 87501

2. **Last Name:** Ortiz **First Name:** Antonio
   Place of birth: Monterrey, Mexico
   Social Security Number: 123-47-9876
   Street Address: 88 LaFlor Place
   City, State, Zip Code: Dallas, TX 75233
3. **Last Name:** Schueler **First Name:** Monica
   Place of birth: Boston, Massachusetts, U.S.A.
   Social Security Number: 432-10-6678
   Street Address: 1400 American Avenue, #7B
   City, State, Zip Code: New York, NY 10019
4. **Last Name:** Bryson **First Name:** Denise
   Place of birth: Québec, Canada
   Social Security Number: 554-32-1234
   Street Address: 771 E. 49th Street, #3
   City, State, Zip Code: Chicago, IL 60618

Unit 11

EXERCISE 3

Suggested answer:

Capital D as in dog, V as in vase, H as in hat, Industries. New line: one two nine three Division Street—that's capital D–i–v–i–s–i–o–n Street. New line: Detroit, Michigan, capital D–e–t–r–o–i–t, space, capital M as in Mouse, capital I. The zip code is four eight two oh one.

EXERCISE 4

Script:

1. Please note that
   Workwell Watches
   788 W. 51st Street
   Washington, D.C. 20003
   is moving to
   17 Cherry Blossom Lane
   Washington, D.C. 20003
   on January 23

2. The Goya Art Gallery
   17 Tamworth Place
   Los Angeles, CA 90025
   Our new address as of March 10 will be
   262 Palmdale Blvd.
   Los Angeles, CA 90028

3. CHANGE OF ADDRESS
   AS OF OCTOBER 13
   Pyramid Sandpapers Inc.
   224 S. Wolf Road
   Birmingham, AL 35402
   IS MOVING TO:
   49 Roosevelt Street
   P.O. Box 464
   Birmingham, AL 35404

Unit 12

EXERCISE 2

1. on the 18th of June
2. at two o'clock
3. on Wednesday
4. in the afternoon
5. on December 25th (on Christmas Day)
6. at night

EXERCISE 4

1. at **2.** at **3.** on **4.** on **5.** in **6.** in

EXERCISE 5

1. Please ask Mr. Smith to meet me <u>at</u> Union Station <u>on</u> May 3rd <u>at</u> 11:00.
2. Terry is <u>in</u> Mexico <u>on</u> a business trip <u>at</u> the silver factory this week.
3. Our phone rings more <u>in</u> the morning than <u>in</u> the afternoon and never <u>in</u> the evening.
4. I'll be <u>in</u> my office or <u>at</u> the conference <u>on</u> Wednesday when you arrive.
5. The company will be closed <u>in</u> August and <u>on</u> Christmas Day.
6. I'm coming <u>to</u> Tokyo <u>on</u> Friday and staying <u>until</u> Tuesday.
7. Please finish this project <u>by</u> the end of the month.
8. Mrs. Brown's secretary is going <u>to</u> the bank before she goes home. (NOTE: no preposition before *home*)

EXERCISE 6

1. at **2.** on **3.** in **4.** at

Unit 13

EXERCISE 1

Script:

1.　　You: Rapide Communications. Good morning.

　　　　Caller: Good morning. Could I speak to Mr. Davidson, <u>please</u>?

　　　　You: <u>Certainly</u>. <u>Could</u> I have your name, <u>please</u>?

　　　　Caller: Mark Schwarz from Dallas.

　　　　You: <u>Hold</u> one moment, Mr. Schwarz.

2.　　You: Mrs. Carleton's secretary. How can I help you?

　　　　Caller: I'd like to speak to Ms. Carleton, please.

　　　　You: <u>I'm sorry.</u> Ms. Carleton is <u>on</u> vacation this week. <u>Would</u> you like to leave a <u>message</u>?

　　　　Caller: Yes, could you ask her to call me when she gets back? My name is Sussman.

　　　　You: Could you <u>spell</u> that, <u>please</u>?

　　　　Caller It's S–U <u>double</u> S–M–A–N.

　　　　You: Thank you, Mr. Sussman. I'll make sure she gets the message.

3.　　You: Extension 230.

　　　　Caller: Oh, I'm sorry. I asked for extension 320.

　　　　You: Hold <u>on</u>, please. I'll <u>transfer</u> you back to the <u>switchboard</u>.

EXERCISE 2

1. g	2. f	3. i	4. j	5. h
6. a	7. b	8. d	9. e	10. c

EXERCISE 3

international code, city code

EXERCISE 4

Script:

1. Thank you for <u>calling</u> Goodkin, Smith, and Associates. I'm sorry. There's <u>no one</u> here to answer your call. If you <u>leave</u> your name and telephone number after the <u>beep</u>, we'll <u>call</u> you back as <u>soon</u> as we can.

2. CPA Incorporated. All lines are currently busy. Please remain on the <u>line</u> and your call will be answered shortly.

3. Mediterranean Tours. Our office is now <u>closed</u> for the day. Our office hours are from 9:30 A.M. until 5:30 P.M. If you <u>would</u> like us to call you <u>back</u>, please leave your name and number after the tone.

EXERCISE 5

1. d   2. f   3. a   4. h   5. b   6. g   7. e   8. c

EXERCISE 6

New Style Wool Sweaters—that's four words: New Style Wool Sweaters, New <u>line</u>: Department KK5/BAF—that's <u>capital</u> K <u>capital</u> K 5 <u>slash</u> <u>capital</u> B <u>capital</u> A <u>capital</u> F. New <u>line</u>: two oh five Bradford Road. New <u>line</u>: Omaha—I'll <u>spell</u> that O–M–A–H–A—Nebraska. The <u>zip code</u> is 61801.

EXERCISE 7

1. please	2. calling (speaking)
3. moment	4. connect
5. message	6. called
7. that name here	8. (wrong) number
9. fax	10. bad

EXERCISE 8

1. in	2. in	3. in	4. at	5. on
6. on	7. on	8. in	9. at	10. on
11. at	12. at	13. on	14. from/to	15. on
16. on	17. on	18. at	19. at	20. for

Unit 14A

EXERCISE 1

1. 5420	2. 9647	3. 7129	4. 1584	5. 6710

EXERCISE 2

1. BCST	2. FWXM	3. ZYHB	4. LOQD	5. JKPU

EXERCISE 3

1. BA 804   2. AF 322   3. TW 209   4. SA 674   5. PA 002

EXERCISE 4

1. CBAO   2. JAXW   3. FEIP   4. YIVM   5. SAJG

Unit 14B

Script: Hello. It's 10 o'clock on Friday the 4th. This is Mr. Black. Black, B–L–A–C–K. I wanted to speak to Mr. Lee, L–E–E. Well, I'll call him back at 5 P.M. Yes, 5:00 this afternoon.

Suggested Message: To Mr. Lee from Mr. Black. He'll call back at 5:00 today.

Unit 15A

EXERCISE 1

1. 72 84 91   2. 63 56 33   3. 96 55 48   4. 80 12 17   5. 53 81 27

EXERCISE 2

1. G   2. C   3. Q   4. S   5. Z

EXERCISE 3

1. 1992   2. 1990   3. 1979   4. 1984   5. 1909

EXERCISE 4

1. 34/AV-Z   2. QS.216-3   3. DH 45 F4

Unit 15B

Script: Hello, Mary. This is Bill. It's 9:00 on Friday. Could you call me back at 11:00? My number is 692-3478. Thank you.

Suggested Message: To Mary from Bill. Call Bill back at 11:00. 692-3478.

Unit 16A

EXERCISE 1

1. E A I E   2. J I E J   3. H A Y V   4. A E B I   5. I V A G

EXERCISE 2

1. 701-5830   2. 185-0159   3. 816-1413   4. 490-1968   5. 220-1270

EXERCISE 3

1. b   2. i   3. y   4. g   5. h

EXERCISE 4

1. 80   2. 17   3. 16   4. 15   5. 30

Unit 16B

Script: Good afternoon. It's Monday the 7th at 12:15. Could you give a message to Mr. Jackson, J–A–C–K–S–O–N? This is Mrs. Cooper, C–O–O–P–E–R. I just wanted to confirm that I'll be coming to the meeting on Friday at 9:30. Please could you send me the BIO 92 documentation by fax? He has the number. Thanks.

Suggested Message: To Mr. Jackson from Mrs. Cooper. Coming to meeting at 9:30 on Friday. Send her BIO 92 doc. by fax.

Unit 17A

EXERCISE 1

1. (308) 482-9119   2. (609) 984-3615   3. (251) 586-2133
4. (713) 699-9107   5. (773) 467-2391

EXERCISE 2

1. July 1989   2. August 1991   3. March 1984
4. February 1988   5. October 1994

EXERCISE 3

1. BU JA SI   2. KL MN FS   3. VI BR AO   4. JE GA IY
5. TB PL SM

EXERCISE 4

1. 8:15   2. 9:30   3. 7:40   4. 8:50   5. 10:10

Unit 17B

Script: Hi! Today's Saturday. The time is 8:30 in the morning. This is Sylvia Conway, C–O–N–W–A–Y. Could you tell Bob Castaneda, C–A–S–T–A–N–E–D–A, to meet me at Henry's Bar, this evening at 8:00? OK? Eight o'clock at Henry's Bar. Would you ask him to call me back to confirm? My number is 249-6834. Thanks.

Suggested Message: To Bob Castaneda from Sylvia Conway. Meet her at Henry's Bar this evening at 8 o'clock. Call back at 249-6834 to confirm.

Unit 18A

EXERCISE 1

1. 7th 4th 12th   2. 14th 22nd 23rd   3. 11th 15th 6th
4. 9th 30th 28th   5. 1st 13th 19th

EXERCISE 2

1. 4:30   2. 10:45   3. 3:30   4. 5:15   5. 9:30

EXERCISE 3

1. 461-9034 2. 819-3472 3. 629-4818 4. 622-4115 5. 173-5206

EXERCISE 4

1. One <u>moment</u>, please.
2. Who's <u>calling</u>, please?
3. May I <u>help</u> you?
4. He's in a <u>meeting</u>.

Unit 18B

Script: Good evening. It's Tuesday at 7 P.M. My name is Mr. Strasser, S–T–R–A–S–S–E–R. I have a message for Mrs. Pandros, P–A–N–D–R–O–S. I need the following documentation. Could you ask her to send me doc. numbers 382A and 382B by fax? I repeat: 382A and 382B. Also tell her that I have organized a conference in Atlanta for the 18th of December. Good-bye.

Suggested Message: To Mrs. Pandros from Mr. Strasser. Send doc numbers 382A and 382B by fax. Conference in Atlanta on December 18.

Unit 19A

EXERCISE 1

1. (341) 952-8477
2. (201) 495-6712
3. (412) 183-9805
4. (605) 210-3139
5. (212) 294-2099

EXERCISE 2

1. BE
2. HI
3. EM
4. GI
5. VB

EXERCISE 3

1. 9:30
2. 2:45
3. 3:15
4. 11:30
5. 11:45

EXERCISE 4

1. 458/RT. AZ
2. DC20 WX/E
3. 2 4 6 SCV. 15
4. D.B.N. 24/D
5. 67332 ASED.3

Unit 19B

Script: Hello. It's the 1st of May at 11:00 A.M. Toronto time. I'm Mr. McCall, M–c–C–A–L–L, and I have a message for Mrs. Henderson, H–E–N–D–E–R–S–O–N. Could you tell her that I'm coming to New York on May 7? Yes, the 7th. I'll be arriving on TWA Flight Number 670, at twenty to five, that's 4:40 at Kennedy Airport. Many thanks.

Suggested Message: To Mrs. Henderson from Mr. McCall. Coming to New York May 7. TWA Flight Number 670. Arrive 4:40 Kennedy Airport.

Unit 20A

EXERCISE 1

1. (224) 776-9100
2. (331) 409-4223
3. (211) 864-1573
4. (445) 819-0003
5. (113) 592-4078

EXERCISE 2

1. 30th   31st   13th
2. 11th   3rd   5th
3. 17th   14th   21st
4. 20th   9th   23rd
5. 22nd   16th   18th

EXERCISE 3

1. 110   2. 280   3. 323   4. 616   5. 790

EXERCISE 4

Here's the name of a place with a great mechanic:

All-Tune Car Repair
101 Newbury Street
Palm Beach, Florida 33480

Unit 20B

Script: Hi! I'm Miss Baker calling from New York. It's August 25 at 4 o'clock my time. My name is Baker, B–A–K–E–R. Could you give a message to Mr. Dupont? Please tell him that I'll be arriving in Paris on September 10. No, sorry, September 9 at twenty to four in the afternoon. Got it? September 9 at 3:40 at CDG Airport. Could you ask him to meet me there? And to confirm by next Monday? Thanks. Bye.

Suggested Message: To Mr. Dupont from Miss Baker. Arriving in Paris on September 9, 3:40 CDG Airport. Meet her. Confirm by next Monday.

Unit 21A

EXERCISE 1

1. San Francisco   2. Tampa   3. Houston
4. Springfield   5. Pittsburgh

EXERCISE 2

1. 2:00   2. 6:30   3. 7:20   4. 3:15   5. 9:25

EXERCISE 3

1. September 8th   2. March 19th   3. June 22nd
4. May 30th   5. January 13th

EXERCISE 4

1. YWV   2. IEA   3. GYJ   4. BVV

Unit 21B

Script: Hello. It's Thursday at 12:30. This is Caroline Barry, B–A–double R–Y. I want to invite Mr. Oshemazi, O–S–H–E–M–A–Z–I, to lunch next week. I'm free on Monday and Tuesday. Oh no, wait a minute. I'm NOT free on Monday . . . or Thursday, but any other day is fine. Could he call me back before 5:30 this afternoon? My number is (561) 982-2200, I repeat (561) 982-2200. Or call me at home this evening at (561) 977-8101, (561) 977-8101.

Suggested Message: To Mr. Oshemazi from Caroline Barry. Invitation to lunch. Not free Monday or Thursday next week. Call by 5:30 this afternoon at (561) 982-2200 or this evening at home at (561) 977-8101.

Unit 22A

EXERCISE 1

1. The invoice was dated 1/16/87.
2. His date of birth is 4/24/35.
3. The date she started was 11/28/92.
4. The date of the contract is 2/15/93.
5. It was installed on 7/7/90.

EXERCISE 2

1. BIN VEN PAD
2. QST RED RID
3. MNB AJL YWB
4. AEI GID JUD
5. HOF LDY BVC

EXERCISE 3

1. I'm arriving at 7:15 P.M.
2. The plane leaves at 8:40.
3. The departure time is 2:10.
4. We'll have to check in by 3:50 at the latest.
5. Is 4:45 the last appointment?

EXERCISE 4

My business address is as follows:

Erikson and Associates, Inc.
13 Swanson Lane
St. Paul, Minnesota 55117

Unit 22B

Script: Good afternoon. It's Wednesday the 12th at 11:30 A.M. This is Joseph Evans, E–V–A–N–S. I have a message for Malcolm MacDonald, M–A–C–capital D–O–N–A–L–D.

I can't come to Portland on July 20. I'm coming on the 25th and staying until the 30th. From the 25th to the 30th. Could you change the date of my meeting from the 22nd to the 26th? So NO meeting on the 22nd. It's on the 26th.

Suggested Message: To Malcolm MacDonald from Joseph Evans. Can't come to Portland July 20. Coming 25th to 30th. Change date of meeting from 22nd to 26th.

Unit 23A

EXERCISE 1

1. My new number is (701) 682-3113.
2. Why not call me at (391) 225-4833?

3. His private line is (734) 616-9113.

4. He's at our Austin office today. The number's (031) 440-1867.

5. Let me find the number. Ah, here it is. It's (802) 775-6193.

EXERCISE 2

1. It's a shipment for Mexico.

2. The raw materials come from Canada.

3. The last conference was in South Korea.

4. The situation in Russia is uncertain at the moment.

5. The last consignment came from China.

EXERCISE 3

1. The first meeting was on September 3, 1990.

2. The Washington office was opened on July 17, 1989.

3. The invoice date is October 4, 1992.

4. Her application form says March 21, 1973.

5. The contract expires on December 31, 1999.

EXERCISE 4

Our travel agent's address is as follows:
Spectacular Holidays
483 Thacker Street
New York, NY 10029

Unit 23B

Script: 11:15 A.M. Monday. I'd like to leave a message for my secretary, Jennifer Buckley, B–U–C–K–L–E–Y. This is Mr. Zetland, Z–E–T–L–A–N–D. I'm in Mali and it's my wife's birthday next week on February 18. Could you ask Jennifer to send her flowers and a card? Here's my wife's name and address: Mrs. Jane Zetland, again, Zetland, 1879 Sioux Avenue, S–I–O–U–X Avenue, Salt Lake City, Utah 84126. Thank you. Good-bye.

Suggested Message: To Jennifer Buckley from Mr. Zetland. Stuck in Mali. Send flowers and birthday card to his wife February 18. Mrs. Jane Zetland, 1879 Sioux Avenue, Salt Lake City, Utah 84126.

Unit 24A

EXERCISE 1

1. We'll have coffee at half past three.

2. The arrival time is 4:20.

3. Call and tell them I'll be there at about ten to seven.

4. I'm sorry to say that your flight arrives in Albany at 2:55 A.M.

5. They said that you'll arrive at five to three in the morning.

EXERCISE 2

1. Chicago O'Hare   2. Boston Logan   3. New York J. F. Kennedy
4. Houston Hobby   5. Washington, D.C. Ronald Reagan National

EXERCISE 3

1. He's out of <u>town</u> this week.   2. Can he call you <u>back</u> at 5 o'clock?
3. The meeting's <u>can</u>celled.   4. What's your ad<u>dress</u>, please?

EXERCISE 4

1. December 25 (Christmas Day)
2. 4th of July (Independence Day)
3. January 1 (New Year's Day)
4. February 14 (Valentine's Day)
5. October 31 (Halloween)

Unit 24B

Script: 5:15. October 1st. Good afternoon. This is Beth Whittle, W–H–I–T–T–L–E calling with a message for Al Curtis, C–U–R–T–I–S. I want to give you the exact times of the meeting on November 3. It begins at half past nine and finishes for lunch at quarter after twelve. So that's 9:30 to 12:15. Then we have lunch at the Strand Palace Hotel. The meeting starts again at two o'clock and ends at quarter to five. OK? Bye.

Suggested Message: To Al Curtis from Beth Whittle. Meeting on November 3 from 9:30 to 12:15. Lunch at the Strand Palace Hotel. Meeting from 2:00 to 4:45.

Unit 25A

EXRCISE 1

1. James (Robertson)   2. Barbara (Lawson)   3. Matthew (Fleming)
4. Felicia (Barber)   5. Jane (Woodfall)

EXERCISE 2

1. I think it's (923) 684-2177.
2. Their new number is 468-3562.
3. (115) 467-7000. Yes, I'm sure it's (115) 467-7000.
4. It's been changed to (907) 333-9426.
5. The code is (302) and the number is 736-3444.

EXERCISE 3

1. The taxi is booked for a quarter to twelve.
2. 10:10. The timetable definitely said ten after ten.
3. Your train leaves at 9:50 from the Central Station.
4. Could you book me a taxi for about 7:35 tomorrow morning?
5. The president is scheduled to arrive at twenty to ten.

EXERCISE 4

Why not take my address. It's

Michael Limited
872 Kilor Street
Ontario, Canada M4W3RB

Unit 25B

Script: Hi! Tuesday, 1:30 P.M. This is John Waters, W–A–T–E–R–S, calling for Jerry Romano, R–O–M–A–N–O. I'm really sorry, but I need to change my order for cable. Please *DON'T* send me 2,000 feet of XL cable. I want 2,500 feet of XXL. So, please send 2,500 feet of XXL cable. Could you call me back at (442) 910-5370? I repeat, (442) 910-5370.

Suggested Message: To Jerry Romano from John Waters. Change order. Not 2,000 feet of XL cable, but 2,500 feet of XXL. Call back (442) 910-5370.

Unit 26A

EXERCISE 1

1. Could you find me the code for San Salvador?
2. Has that fax come in yet from Singapore?
3. Our office in Buenos Aires is on the line.
4. I have a call for you. Mr. Numoto in Tokyo.
5. Do you know what time it is in Vancouver?

EXERCISE 2

1. We opened your account on March 1, 1991.
2. The contract expired on February 3, 1989.
3. The date of renewal is January 11, 1994.
4. His birthday is May 2.
5. He died on September 1, 1992.

EXERCISE 3

1. I have half past one.
2. There's a meeting in the board room at 2:00 P.M.
3. We'll have a short break at a quarter after ten.
4. The quarter to two train gets in too late.
5. The meeting must finish by 7:30.

EXERCISE 4

We've just opened a new office in Tennessee. The address is as follows:

Buro Felts
1798 W. 41st Avenue
Nashville, TN 37205

Unit 26B

Script: February 10 at 2:30. Good afternoon. My name is Miss Cole, C–O–L–E and I'm calling to speak to your Mr. Hernandez. There's a problem on your invoice number 4926, that's invoice 4926, dated the 30th, no—the 31st of January. The amount on the invoice is $8,752.50 plus tax. There's a mistake and it should read $8,725.00 plus tax. Could you (correct) the invoice and send us a new one? So, it's invoice 4926 and it should be for $8,725.00. Thank you.

Suggested Message: To Mr. Hernandez from Miss Cole. Problem on invoice no. 4926 dated January 31. Amount on invoice $8,752.50 plus tax. Should be $8,725.00 plus tax. Correct and send new invoice.

Unit 27A

EXERCISE 1

1. 22,617   2. 48,170   3. 70,001   4. 42,310   5. 90,919

EXERCISE 2

1. (John) Coleman   2. (Kyle) Lindholm   3. (Andrea) Michelson
4. (Peter) Cusak   5. (Antonio) Alvarez

EXERCISE 3

1. Today's date is August 30, 1992.
2. The documents must be in the mail by May 13.
3. Could you get me a flight to Budapest on March 6?
4. The one-day conference is on April 26.
5. There will be a celebration on May 31.

EXERCISE 4

1. I'll put you <u>through</u>.   2. I'd like to speak to Mr. Im<u>a</u>ri, please.
3. I'm afraid he's <u>out</u> all afternoon.   4. What time will he be a<u>vail</u>able?

Unit 27B

Script: Good morning. It's 9:30 on Tuesday, the 13th. My name is Lydia Dalton, that's spelled D–A–L–T–O–N. I'm calling for Mr. Morris, M–O–R–R–I–S. Could you give him a message for me, please? I'm sorry, but we can't deliver the SBN order until March. We have SBK in stock at the moment and can deliver it to you by Friday. If you accept the SBK, we'll offer you a 15% discount to compensate. Could you ask Mr. Morris to call back today? My number is 388-0421, extension 556.

Suggested Message: To Mr. Morris from Lydia Dalton. Can't deliver SBN until March. SBK in stock and can be delivered by Friday. 15% discount to compensate. Call back today 388-0421, extension 556.

Unit 28A

EXERCISE 1

1. The order was for 2,844.
2. We counted, but there were only 26,008.
3. That was 17,659, not 70.
4. The initial order will be for 13,000.
5. We can supply 6,142 immediately from stock.

EXERCISE 2

1. Can Mr. Welsh make the meeting on July 17th?
2. He won't be back in the country until May 7th.
3. The contract expires on December 31st.
4. We're closed for vacation from August 1st.
5. We reopen on August 21st.

EXERCISE 3

1. We're planning on catching the 2:35 to Paris Charles de Gaulle.
2. That means we'll be arriving about 3:25.
3. We hope to be back in the hotel by about twenty to seven.
4. The night train leaves at 10:35.
5. It's now five after eleven, so let's have a break.

EXERCISE 4

Here's the address of a good contact in Mexico:

Electronics Mexicanos
42 Avenida Grande
CP 07500
Mexico, DF

Unit 28B

Script: Hello. It's 9:30 P.M. on Wednesday the 25th. This is Tony Waller, W–A–L–L–E–R. I'd like to speak to Jack Springfield, S–P–R–I–N–G–F–I–E–L–D, or leave him a message. I liked the samples he sent me and I'd like to place an order. Please send me 2 boxes of Y20 film, 1 box of Y30 film, and 1 box of X32 film. I'll repeat that: 2 boxes of Y20, 1 box of Y30, and 1 box of X32 film. Oh, and I need them as soon as possible.

Suggested Message: To Jack Springfield from Tony Waller. Liked sample of films. Wants to place an order. 2 boxes of Y20, 1 box of Y30, and 1 box of X32 as soon as possible.